Hypnosis: Self Hypnosis -

Control Your Mind - Control Your Life

Have Complete Control Over Your Mind And Reduce Stress With Proven Techniques

Table Of Contents

Introduction

You are about to make a startling new discovery - one that will transform your world. The ancient technique described in this book has been around for hundreds of years, and it has nothing to do with the occult and everything to do with the power of the mind!

The Ancient Egyptians used this technique in something they called sleep temples because they knew that the mind and the body were inextricably linked. The Greeks also used this simple technique in their healing shrines and this technique has played an active role in helping people manifest change since the beginning of time.

This discovery forms a powerful bridge that permits science and spirituality to come together, and you can use this discovery to completely transform your life.

In case you are wondering what this discovery is, you must first understand that you are already using it. Every time you turn on the television or get lost in thought, you are using this technique. All you really need to do to transform your life is to focus on exactly what it is you want to create. It's really that simple. You have everything you need already inside you.

In this book, you will learn the age-old technique of hypnosis in an easy to understand manner. With the help of this book, you can use this technique to manifest anything you desire!

Hypnosis is a tool that can make you a manifesting genius. This book covers all the basics including the science behind hypnosis, the benefits of hypnosis, how to use hypnosis to ease away stress and anxiety and how to use it to stop smoking and lose weight, amongst other things.

When you make self-hypnosis a daily habit, there is nothing you cannot accomplish.

The only limitations you have are within your own mind. If you choose to break free, your world will start expanding. When you take responsibility for your life, you begin to connect with your own inner resources.

If you will allow me to take you on this journey, I am honored to be your guide. Welcome to the wonderful world of hypnosis!

within this book are for clarifying purposes only and are the owned by the owners themselves, not affiliated with this document.

What is Hypnosis?

Have you ever wondered if hypnosis was real? Franz Anton Mesmer (1734 – 1815) was actually one of the first scientists to propose a rational basis for the effects of hypnosis.

Mesmer's early theories were based on the idea that there were physical forces in the universe that had some kind of influence on the human body. He based his theories on something called animal magnetism, which inferred that the planets affected humans through a sort of invisible fluid, which could be derived from magnets. Although Mesmer was later ostracized for his theory, his work set the stage for future research to be done.

Doctor James Braid continued the work started by Mesmer, even though he basically rejected the idea of animal magnetism, suggesting instead that hypnosis was a form of sleep.

James Braid was actually the first person to coin the phrase "hypnosis" leading the way for future research in the field. Braid was also the first physician to suggest that hypnosis could be induced by the simple act of the patient staring at a fixed object, a method still used today.

James Esdaile, a Scottish doctor in Calcutta, India in the mid-1800, performed thousands of operations utilizing only hypnosis for anesthesia, which is quite amazing. Although there was no scientific explanation for why this worked, there was a drop in the fatality rate from 25% to a mere 5%.

Hypnotherapy has been used in Dental Practice as far back as the 19th century and The American Medical Association got on board as well in 1958, approving a report on the medical usage of hypnosis.

Although the AMA later rescinded all of their policies instated from 1881-1958, some well-deserved recognition came when the American Psychological Association advocated hypnosis as an actual subsidiary of psychology a few years after the AMA approval.

One of the most famous psychiatrists to use hypnosis was Milton Erickson, a 20th Century therapist. He changed the way hypnosis was used by using persuasive language patterns leading the way for further research and development utilizing hypnosis.

With modern day advances in brain imaging and neurological science, hypnosis has come a long way and gained a lot of respect as well.

Whatever the history behind it, hypnosis is an incredible process. It can help you overcome challenges you have spent a lifetime fighting and it can help you literally change your life, all with the power of your thoughts.

In light of all of this, we can safely say hypnosis is indeed real.

Is Hypnosis And Self Hypnosis Safe?

Yes, hypnosis is a very safe process, because your mind is always in control. Hypnosis cannot make you do anything that goes against your morals or values. Your mind actually drifts in and out of different states of trance on a regular basis every time you daydream or get lost in thought.

Your subconscious mind holds the key to making changes that last. All of those little thoughts you think about all day long basically create your life. Most of us focus on the problems and those things we aren't happy with.

You can guess what happens when you focus on the negative can't you? That's right, more of the negative comes in.

If you dwell on those things that aggravate or annoy you, that's what comes into your life. It's really very simple.

Self-hypnosis is a tool that gives you access to your subconscious mind. It's really as simple as that. If you want to change something in your life, all you really need to do is program in new thoughts.

Cautions and Contra-indications

Before you get started, it is important to set a few ground rules. When doing self-hypnosis, you want to make sure you are free from drugs or alcohol. Those that are under the influence of drugs or alcohol may have a difficult time achieving trance and relaxing.

It is also recommended that those with epilepsy not be hypnotized as well because the state of hypnosis could elicit seizures - but only for those who currently have epilepsy. In addition, hypnosis may not be suitable if you have a heart condition, extremely high blood pressure or a psychosis or mental illness. In the case where you have a chronic health condition you may choose to seek approval from your health care provider just to be on the safe side. It is also important to avoid caffeine immediately prior to a hypnosis session.

There are many ways to induce a light state of trance. It is important to realize that even light levels of hypnosis can be very effective because you don't need to be in a deep state of trance to elicit change.

Hypnosis helps you be the best you can be. It is really a very natural process and a process that can transform your life.

Your mind is an incredible tool, but sometimes it takes a little time to make changes. If you have spent a lifetime immersed in turmoil and drama, it may take a little time to get your mind moving in a different direction.

Your mind is like an old chalkboard; everything you have even known is written on it. Using hypnosis, or self-hypnosis you can begin to erase those old worn out behaviors and program new ones into your life.

What could be simpler than that?

Types of Hypnosis

You might be wondering at this point what the difference is between self-hypnosis, NLP (Neuro-linguistic programming), hypnotherapy and everything else.

There are several different methods when it comes to programming the mind, and it is important to have a basic understanding of what these methods are.

With traditional hypnosis, you are basically offering the mind suggestions. Within hypnosis there is:

- Direct Suggestions or Autosuggestion.

- Indirect Suggestions.

- Ericksonian Hypnosis or Story Telling Using Metaphors.

- Embedded Commands.

- NLP - Neuro Linguistic Programming.

- Conversational Hypnosis.

- Subliminal Programming.

Direct Suggestions

Direct suggestions or autosuggestion is a very popular method of hypnosis. With this kind of hypnosis, the hypnotist gives the client direct suggestions while in trance. These suggestions could be anything you like, related to your dream or goal.

However, if you are one of those types of people who are overly critical or analytical, direct suggestions may not work for you.

Indirect Suggestions.

Indirect suggestions are suggestions that are hidden within a story or a suggestion that isn't quite as obvious. Indirect suggestions are a great way to get past the conscious thinking mind because there is no conflict when it comes to believability.

Ericksonian Hypnosis

Ericksonian Hypnosis, or hypnosis derived from Milton Erickson, uses stories or colorful metaphors to help people make changes. Erickson believed in using stories to help people heal, and he was quite famous for them. Stories are a wonderful way to overcome resistance because they tend to be more believable than a direct suggestion.

Embedded commands

Embedded commands are suggestions used within the guise of a story and they are used as kind of a softening language. Embedded commands may use language such as "You probably already know that ____" or "I'm wondering if you'll ____ or not?"

Embedded commands help the hypnotist bypass the conscious mind, and they can very effective.

NLP - Neuro Linguistic Programming

Another type of programming used frequently is NLP or neuro-linguistic programming. NLP combines different aspects of behavioral psychology, hypnosis, linguistics, modeling and common sense.

NLP is a method of influencing the behavior of the brain through the usage of language and other kinds of communication that helps someone recode the way their brain responds to stimuli or programming to manifest better and new behaviors.

There are many distinct methods within NLP, including rapport, behavioral modeling, the Meta model, etc.

Conversational Hypnosis

Conversational Hypnosis, also known as Covert hypnosis isn't used as much as some of the more traditional methods. Covert hypnosis can be very effective when it comes to sales, and it does have a valid reason for its existence.

Subliminal Programming.

Subliminal Programming can be very effective as well. In subliminal programming, the suggestions are hidden and not heard by the conscious mind. The theory behind this type of programming is that the subconscious is aware and can hear the suggestions, even though, the conscious mind cannot.

Hypnosis Benefits

Many people use self-hypnosis to achieve goals and to promote healing. Guided Imagery, which is a form of trance, is used all of the time in the Health Care System to help patients visualize themselves healing, and self-hypnosis is very similar.

With hypnosis you can:
- Make changes must faster.
- Manage Stress Better.
- Stop Smoking.
- Lose Weight.
- Overcome Addictions.
- Be More Successful.
- Heal Your Body.

- Improve Your Life.
- Think More Positively.
- Embrace Change.
- Supercharge Confidence.
- Be More Prosperous.

Why You Should incorporate Self-Hypnosis Into Your Daily Life

When you engage in a regular self-hypnosis program you can better manage stress and anxiety and live a healthier life. Hypnosis helps you do everything better, and that's really the beauty of it.

Hypnosis is by far one of the easiest ways there is to make changes in your life, and you can do a simple self-hypnosis program in 15-20 minutes a day. Hypnosis is like a process that can help you make amazing changes in your life in an easy and reliable manner.

I'm Skeptical Would Hypnosis Really Work For Me?

Yes, it works. Hypnosis is a very gentle process, and one that is extremely effective and very relaxing.

Learning how to do self-hypnosis can completely transform your life. Your thoughts become things, and using hypnosis, you can literally train your mind to focus on whatever it is you want to create.

Step-by-Step Guide To Hypnotizing Yourself

Self-hypnosis really only requires three things to be successful:

- The ability to relax.

- The motivation to make change.

- Positive suggestions.

The only real difference between hypnosis and self-hypnosis is that in hypnosis, you permit the hypnotist to bring about a state of relaxation; in self-hypnosis the relaxation portion is self-induced.

When you relax into hypnosis, you will become drowsy, your eyes will feel heavy and you will feel a delightful sense of relaxation coming over you. This is a natural state many of us experience prior to falling asleep. Self-hypnosis simply allows you to produce that state of mind artificially, prolonging it to your advantage.

If you can relax and follow some simple instructions, you can hypnotize yourself.

In order to practice self-hypnosis it is important to learn how to visualize. Visualization is a very powerful tool and one that can help you supercharge your self-hypnosis sessions. We all visualize in different ways, so don't get discouraged if you can't "see" something in your mind.

Your mind processes things differently depending on whether or not you sense things in a visual, auditory or a kinesthetic manner. This is also known as VAK.

Each of us sees things from a different perspective. During hypnosis, you may see, sense or even hear things. Not everyone sees colorful pictures in their mind, and that's OK be-

17

cause if you sense something, or imagine hearing something, that's just as valid.

You can visualize in many different ways, so don't restrict yourself to one mode versus another, just see where your mind takes you.

Visualization is a gentle but powerful technique that focuses and directs the imagination. The only requirement to make visualization work for you is the use of your imagination.

Try this visualization process now:

Find a quiet place to sit or lie down. Start some deep breathing or tense & relax your muscles. Let all your thoughts go by acknowledging them and then releasing them.

Now imagine a beautiful beach. See yourself walking along this beach and sinking your toes into the sand. Feel the cool water and the ocean breeze. See if you can taste the salty sea air. Listen for the sounds of the waves. Look up into the sky and notice the colors. Notice the color of the water. Step into the water, and notice how soothing the water feels.

You can imagine anything. Use all of your senses and see, feel and be there in your mind. Allow it to look like and feel like just the way you want it to, and if it doesn't happen- just make it up. Whatever you imagine, imagine it with all your senses.

Notice how warm or cold it is. Notice what it smells like. Notice how it feels to your touch. Feel the warmth of the sunshine on your back. Listen for any sounds and notice if they are in rhythm with your breathing. There is no right or wrong way to practice visualization, so don't worry!

Make sure and take time every day to close your eyes and spend a few moments visualizing yourself living the life of your dreams. Visualization is a very powerful tool, especially when you combine it with affirmations.

Eye-Fixation Self-Hypnosis Induction

Relax and get comfortable and find a quiet place to sit or lie down. Uncross your arms and your legs. Take a long, slow deep breath, feeling your breath as it enters your body. As you exhale, your body releasing toxins, stress and negativity.

Now focus your eyes on something above your head, like on a spot on the wall or the ceiling. You are attempting to strain your eyes so try and keep your eyes open and focused upward as long as you can.

As you strain your eyes, slowly count backward from 100 - 1. Once you finally close your eyes, you will already be in a light level of hypnosis. Don't worry if you get tired and don't want to finish counting backward; that's the idea.

As you count backward, allow yourself to drift into a state of deep relaxation.

When you get to the point where you cannot keep your eyes open, close them gently as you let your attention drift.

You may then proceed with your visualization or self-hypnosis session of your choice.

Once you finish your self-hypnosis, tell yourself that the suggestions are firmly embedded into your subconscious mind where they grow stronger and stronger each and every day.

Make sure and visualize yourself 6 months down the road, having already achieved success. Notice how different you are in this new state of mind. This part of the process is very powerful so take a few moments to see yourself resolved of the situation or issue.

When you are finished, simply count yourself up from 1 to 5.

Staircase Induction

Relax and get comfortable and find a quiet place to sit or lie down. Uncross your arms and your legs. Continue breathing deeply until you feel your energy calming.

Begin by imagining yourself at the top of a beautiful staircase, visualizing one you may have seen at a beautiful house or a museum. Slowly count yourself down at least 5 -10 stairs. Imagine with each step that you become lighter and lighter as you go deeper and deeper. You may also choose to count backward from 100-1, stopping whenever you feel a place of deep relaxation.

As you move down the stairs, feel your feet becoming softer and lighter, as you travel. If you lose the intention to continue going down the stairs, you may either give yourself some positive suggestions or just relax.

Proceed with your self-hypnosis session.

When you are finished, tell yourself that the suggestions are firmly embedded into your subconscious mind where they will grow stronger and stronger each and every day.

Make sure and visualize yourself 6 months down the road, having already achieved your goals. This part of the process is very powerful so take a few moments to see yourself resolved of the situation or issue.

When you are finished, you can take yourself back up the stairway, as you count from 1 to 5

Helpful Tips for Relaxation

There are some simple phrases you can repeat in your mind to help you achieve a light state of trance. Some common ones include:

- The deeper I go the better I feel and the better I feel the deeper I go.

- I allow the soothing sound of my voice to calm and relax me.

- Moment by moment, my mind is becoming as clear as the surface of a calm and quiet lake.

- As I continue to breathe deeply, I become more and more relaxed, more and more at ease.

- I allow my body to become more and more relaxed with each passing moment.

- Every sound that I hear allows me to go deeper and deeper into hypnotic trance.

- It's easy for me to relax deeply.

- Breathing deeply brings me into a deep state of relaxation.

- I am at peace.

- I am calm and relaxed.

- I easily achieve a very deep state of relaxation.

- Each and every muscle of my body is now relaxing.

- I am now in a deep state of relaxation and going deeper and deeper.

You may either choose to repeat a few of these phrases to help you relax or you may simply choose one phrase, repeating it over and over. Choosing a phrase like "I am at peace" or "I am calm and relaxed" works well too, because it gives your mind something to focus on.

Once you are in a deep state of relaxation, just give your mind some positive suggestions that reflect the state of mind you are aiming for. You may also want to use this time to visualize yourself having already achieved your goals.

Deepening scripts

A hypnotic deepener helps you double your relaxation and drift farther into trance.

Place of Peace deepening script.

Begin by imagining a place where no one can bother you and no one can find you. You might be lying on a beautiful beach or at some kind of secluded hideaway.

Allow yourself to use all of your senses to enjoy everything around you. Feel the warm air, sense the sand or the ground under you feet and smell the beautiful fragrances.

Notice how beautiful everything is and how relaxed you feel. Just continue breathing deeply and allowing this feeling of relaxation to take over. Imagine what might be around you, like beautiful plants or flowers. Imagine how fresh every-thing is. Feel the air against your skin and the sun on your face.

Bonus: Your Own Self-Hypnosis Scripts

Each of these scripts includes a *trigger word*, which will help you relax and focus on your issue.

Try this eyes open hypnosis by reading this script out loud.

Alternatively you can pre record these scripts in any audio. Most computers have audio recording software that can make this process with ease.

Another option would simply be using the voice recorder your smart phone to pre record these scripts, so you can sit back and just enjoy your own voice taking you into trance.

Ease Away Stress and Anxiety

Begin by relaxing and getting into a comfortable position. Just read the script out loud allowing your words to flow into your consciousness.

Feeling a sense of peace, I allow the soothing sound of my voice to lull me into a sort of hypnotic trance. I am speaking softly and slowly, as I go deeper and deeper into this beautiful state of trance. My voice and my body are slowing down, as though everything is in slow motion. With every word I speak, and every sound I make, I go deeper and deeper into a state of hypnotic trance. Moment by moment, my mind is becoming clearer and clearer, as smooth as the surface of a beautiful lake.

As my mind clears, ***I am at peace, I am at peace.***

I use my imagination to relax even more deeply. As I speak, I imagine myself walking along a beautiful beach.

As I walk, I can hear the sounds of the waves hitting the shore and I can feel the sea breeze as it touches my nose. I take deep and cleansing breaths, which helps me go deeper and deeper into this beautiful relaxation.

I feel the sea breeze drift over my body, and I notice the sun as it warms my skin. The sun touches me wherever I have tension or stress, instantly dissolving anything it finds. This beautiful healing light allows me to go even deeper into this beautiful sense of relaxation. All of my stress and tension is now dissolving, as I go deeper and deeper. Every time I speak the words, deeper and deeper, I will go into a deep state of hypnotic trance.

I feel myself moving deeper and deeper down, as I begin to count backward from five to one.

Number five.........I feel very calm and relaxed.

Number four........I'm moving down deeper and deeper.

Number three......deeper still.

Number two...........I feel myself descending ever deeper now. And on the next number, I will drift into a very deep state of relaxation. And......

Number one...........I am in a very deep state of relaxation, and I am ready to make some amazing changes in my life.

I am at peace, I am at peace.

As I relax on this beach, I realize that this day has changed me. I am now feeling very relaxed, as I continue to go even deeper. As I walk on this beautiful beach, I hear the sound of the waves hitting the shoreline - I notice the feeling of the sun on my skin.

In the background I hear the gentle, rhythmic sound of the breeze as it blows over the sand. I can taste the saltiness as the air cleanses my skin. As I continue to breathe deeply, I become aware of other sensations, and sounds. Here on this beach I am free from stress, and in touch with the calm power within me. The sun feels warm on my face and it feels good. My mind feels completely free and uncluttered.

As I walk along the beach, I notice how warm the sand feels on my feet. Walking a little further, I stop for a moment to take in the feeling of the warm, clean air on my skin. As I stand on the beach, I enjoy watching the water - I notice all of the different colors that make up the ocean.

No one is around, so I decide to sit down and enjoy the view. As I relax, I feel as if a weight has been lifted from my shoulders. The breeze is blowing away all of the stress that is left in my body, leaving me feeling refreshed and invigorated.

The air on this beautiful beach is transforming me and as I relax. I realize I now easily handle anything that comes at me day by day. I realize I can achieve anything now, because stress does not rule my life.

As I rest and relax, I repeat the following statements:

- I choose to feel relaxed and positive.

- Every breath I take relaxes me.

- I am at peace.

- I am empowered.

- I easily let go of stress.

- I choose to be peaceful in the moment.

- I have a sense of balance in my life.

- I am an unlimited being.

- Challenges help me grow.

- I am filled with peace, hope and joy.

This incredible place has changed my life, and I am now ready for a new journey where I will meet new people and accomplish amazing things.

These suggestions are now firmly embedded into my subconscious mind, where they will grow stronger and stronger each and every day.

I now bring myself back to a full waking consciousness at the count of 5. When I get to the number five I will feel well rested, wide-awake and completely refreshed and ready to take on the rest of my day or evening.

#1 ....Just beginning to come back now... feeling the energy coming back into my body.

#2 ....Coming back more and more, knowing that a transformation has already begun.

#3 ....Now I am really coming back to the present moment. I can begin to feel my body wanting to stretch and move and come back.

#4............Coming back even more now. Breathing in a deep breath of waking energy, waking up each and every cell in my body.

#5...........I am now completely wide-awake.

Quit Smoking in its Tracks

Begin with either the eye-fixation induction or the staircase induction. You can also repeat this read a loud induction if you like that.

Feeling a sense of peace, I allow the soothing sound of my voice to lull me into a sort of hypnotic trance. I am speaking softly and slowly, as I go deeper and deeper into this beautiful state of trance. My voice and my body are slowing down, as though everything is in slow motion. With every word I speak, and every sound I make, I go deeper and deeper into a state of hypnotic trance. Moment by moment, my mind is becoming clearer and clearer, as smooth as the surface of a beautiful lake.

As my mind clears, *I am free, I am free.*

I use my imagination to relax even more deeply. As I speak, I imagine myself walking in a beautiful meadow.

As I walk, I can feel the breeze as it touches my nose. I take deep and cleansing breaths, which helps me go deeper and deeper into this beautiful relaxation.

I notice the sun as it warms my skin. The sun touches me wherever I have tension or stress, instantly dissolving anything it finds. I can smell the aroma of beautiful plants and flowers. *I am free, I am free.*

This beautiful healing light allows me to go even deeper into a sense of relaxation. All of my stress and tension is now dissolving, as I go deeper and deeper. Every time I speak the words, deeper and deeper, I will go into a deep state of hypnotic trance.

I feel myself moving deeper and deeper down, as I begin to count backward from five to one.

Number five.........I feel very calm and relaxed.

Number four........I'm moving down deeper and deeper.

Number three......deeper still.

Number two...........I feel myself descending ever deeper now. And on the next number, I will drift into a very deep state of relaxation. And......

Number one...........I am in a very deep state of relaxation, and I am ready to make some amazing changes in my life.

I am free, I am free.

As I relax more and more, I realize that I do not need to smoke. I now have a strong desire to be healthy, and to have more energy. I breathe easily and deeply and I am in control.

As I take control of my life and my health, I am free of cigarettes and free of all tobacco. I am also free to enjoy my life more. I like feeling healthy and vibrant. I look better and feel better and everyone notices.

I am proud that I am leaving behind an unhealthy, unnatural habit, and proud that I now have greater respect for myself.

I am free, I am free.

I hear myself refusing cigarettes when they are offered to me....and I see myself saying to people "No thanks, I don't smoke."

I enjoy the feeling of freedom......I like feeling this freedom. I enjoy being able to breathe deeply, I enjoy smelling fresh and clean. I notice my teeth are whiter and my breath is fresher. I am healthier in every way.

The only substitute I need is a long slow deep breath, and fresh clean air. I like this new freedom....*I am free, I am free.*

Every day I am more and more determined to be a non-smoker, and I am a non-smoker and will be for the rest of my life.

I have made the decision not to smoke. I have decided to give myself permission not to smoke. I have made up my mind and decided to change. I am tired of being bullied around - and it stops NOW.

I am in control of my life, and that is that. There is no activity in life that goes better with cigarettes, and now I know. So, from this moment on, it's going to be very easy for me because I have decided not to smoke and I have lost the desire for tobacco in any form, at anytime, at any place, under any conditions, in any situation.

Not smoking is a wonderful new way of life for me. I congratulate myself on my decision not to smoke, and I will remain a non-smoker for the rest of my life from this moment forward.

My body thanks me.

I am free, I am free.

I see myself 6 months down the road, as a healthy non-smoker, and I like what I see. I look healthy, because I am healthy.

These suggestions are now firmly embedded into my subconscious mind, where they will grow stronger and stronger each and every day.

I now bring myself back to a full waking consciousness at the count of 5. When I get to the number five I will feel well rested, wide-awake and completely refreshed and ready to take on the rest of my day or evening.

#1 ....Just beginning to come back now... feeling the energy coming back into my body.

#2 ....Coming back more and more, knowing that a transformation has already begun.

#3 ....Now I am really coming back to the present moment. I can begin to feel my body wanting to stretch and move and come back.

#4............Coming back even more now. Breathing in a deep breath of waking energy, waking up each and every cell in my body.

#5...........I am now completely wide-awake.

You may repeat your trigger word, ***I am free, I am free,*** anytime you feel the craving for a cigarette, and the craving will go away.

Beliefs of Geniuses

Simply repeat the following statements to relax.

The deeper I go the better I feel and the better I feel the deeper I go. I allow the soothing sound of my voice to calm and relax me. Moment by moment, my mind is becoming as clear as the surface of a calm and quiet lake. As I continue to breathe deeply, I become more and more relaxed, more and more at ease.

I allow my body to become more and more relaxed with each passing moment. Every sound that I hear allows me to go deeper and deeper into hypnotic trance. It's easy for me to relax deeply.

Breathing deeply brings me into a deep state of relaxation. I am at peace.

I am calm and relaxed. I easily achieve a very deep state of relaxation. Each and every muscle of my body is now relaxing.

I am a creative genius. I know that true intelligence is accomplished by the interplay of both the left and right hemispheres of my brain. I can boost my intelligence by tapping into the ability to use both sides of my brain at the same time.

Tapping into my super IQ is actually quite easy. My brain is the most powerful bio-computer on the planet and it is capable of some incredible feats. I have the ability to increase my brain's neuroplasticity by using my left brain and right brain simultaneously.

It's easy for me to think like a genius, because I now take on the beliefs of a genius. This new belief has given me many advantages in my life. Being a creative genius is easy for me. I recognize that the true geniuses of this world were very special, as I am special.

I know that everything I do starts in the mind, and I have a very creative intelligent mind. I think like a genius thinks, and it's an effortless process.

When I unlock this potential, I can accomplish anything. When I tap into this Super IQ I upgrade my brain per se so that I can more easily absorb new information. This kind of super learning power is accessible for everyone and once I flip that switch, I will be unstoppable.

I know my brain has the ability to rewire itself, and it has the ability to tap into the beliefs of geniuses. I can easily train my brain to think like a genius, and I do.

Everything in my life is changing and improving because of my new ability.

I think like a genius, because I am a genius.

I see myself as a very smart individual. I now imagine how my life has changed, because of this new ability. I now get whatever I want, because of this ability. It's easy for me to boost my intelligence, and I am doing so right now.

I think like a genius, because I am a genius.

I now tap into the flow available to everyone, the flow of creative thought. I allow for greater mental clarity. I have boosted my intelligence. I like to think of myself as a genius, because I am a genius.

Every time I speak these words, I tap into this ability more and more.

I think like a genius, because I am a genius.

Everything in my life is improving, because of this new ability.

I like who I am becoming. People notice my new abilities. I have more success, better relationships and vibrant health because of my new ability.

I think like a genius, because I am a genius and it is so.

These suggestions are now firmly embedded into my subconscious mind, where they will grow stronger and stronger each and every day.

I now bring myself back to a full waking consciousness at the count of 5. When I get to the number five I will feel well rested, wide-awake and completely refreshed and ready to take on the rest of my day or evening.

#1 ....Just beginning to come back now... feeling the energy coming back into my body.

#2 ....Coming back more and more, knowing that a transformation has already begun.

#3 ....Now I am really coming back to the present moment. I can begin to feel my body wanting to stretch and move and come back.

#4............Coming back even more now. Breathing in a deep breath of waking energy, waking up each and every cell in my body.

#5...........I am now completely wide-awake.

Create An Indestructible Shield from Negativity

Simply repeat the following statements to relax.

The deeper I go the better I feel and the better I feel the deeper I go. I allow the soothing sound of my voice to calm and relax me. Moment by moment, my mind is becoming as clear as the surface of a calm and quiet lake. As I continue to breathe deeply, I become more and more relaxed, more and more at ease.

I allow my body to become more and more relaxed with each passing moment. Every sound that I hear allows me to go deeper and deeper into hypnotic trance. It's easy for me to relax deeply.

Breathing deeply brings me into a deep state of relaxation. I am at peace.

I am calm and relaxed. I easily achieve a very deep state of relaxation. Each and every muscle of my body is now relaxing.

From this moment forward, I am creating a powerful shield of protection. This protective shield is like a coat of armor around my body. I am indestructible because of it.

This shield of positivity allows only good things in - it repels the rest. Everything in my life is improving because of this powerful force I carry around.

I am powerfully positive, I am powerfully positive.

I see myself as a powerful co-creator in my own life. I imagine this shield like a bubble surrounding my body. I carry this protection wherever I go. This shield of protection attracts good things into my life.

I am powerfully positive, I am powerfully positive.

I see myself walking down the street, with this invisible cloak of protection. I smile because I know how powerful I am. This protection is magnificent; everything good comes into my life.

Nothing negative is allowed in, I repel negativity. I repel anything that does not support my highest good. Every day in every way, I am getting better and better. I release everything bad and take on everything good.

I am more productive and positive. I am powerfully positive.

I allow the universe to deliver whatever I need, want and desire. I allow good things into my life. I repel the bad. This shield of protection follows me everywhere I go. I have faith that I am protected all the time.

I am powerfully positive, I am powerfully positive.

I feel incredible. I deserve the best in life. I believe I am powerfully protected. I can and do have it all.

Anytime I speak to someone, I absorb only the good, I repel the rest. This cloak of protection allows me to live an abundant life.

I am powerfully positive, I am powerfully positive, and it is so.

I now bring myself back to a full waking consciousness at the count of 5. When I get to the number five I will feel well rested, wide-awake and completely refreshed and ready to take on the rest of my day or evening.

#1 ....Just beginning to come back now... feeling the energy coming back into my body.

#2 ....Coming back more and more, knowing that a transformation has already begun.

#3 ....Now I am really coming back to the present moment. I can begin to feel my body wanting to stretch and move and come back.

#4............Coming back even more now. Breathing in a deep breath of waking energy, waking up each and every cell in my body.

#5...........I am now completely wide-awake.

Lose Weight Effortlessly

Begin by relaxing and getting into a comfortable position. Just read the script out loud allowing your words to flow into your consciousness.

Feeling a sense of peace, I allow the soothing sound of my voice to lull me into a sort of hypnotic trance. I am speaking softly and slowly, as I go deeper and deeper into this beautiful state of trance. My voice and my body are slowing down, as though everything is in slow motion. With every word I speak, and every sound I make, I go deeper and deeper into a state of hypnotic trance. Moment by moment, my mind is becoming clearer and clearer, as smooth as the surface of a beautiful lake.

As my mind clears I know, ***I am now my perfect size, I am now my perfect size.***

I use my imagination to relax even more deeply. As I speak, I imagine myself walking along a beautiful beach.

As I walk, I can hear the sounds of the waves hitting the shore and I can feel the sea breeze as it touches my nose. I take deep and cleansing breaths, which helps me go deeper and deeper into this beautiful relaxation.

I feel the sea breeze drift over my body, and I notice the sun as it warms my skin. The sun touches me wherever I have tension or stress, instantly dissolving anything it finds. This beautiful healing light allows me to go even deeper into this beautiful sense of relaxation. All of my stress and tension is now dissolving, as I go deeper and deeper. Every time I speak the words, deeper and deeper, I will go into a deep state of hypnotic trance.

I feel myself moving deeper and deeper down, as I begin to count backward from five to one.

Number five.........I feel very calm and relaxed.

Number four.........I'm moving down deeper and deeper.

Number three......deeper still.

Number two...........I feel myself descending ever deeper now. And on the next number, I will drift into a very deep state of relaxation. And......

Number one...........I am in a very deep state of relaxation, and I am ready to make some amazing changes in my life.

I am now deeply relaxed.......and ready to make some amazing changes in my life. I am taking on a new healthy attitude today. I know it's a smart choice to develop healthy lifestyle habits.....habits that I can continue for a lifetime. I am ready for a strong, fit body and I am making an important commitment towards my good health today.

As you continue to relax.........I imagine my perfect body. This is actually quite easy for me to do because I have spent a lot of time thinking about weight loss. Now that I have chosen hypnosis, I know that weight loss is an effortless process. It's simply a matter of choice. All I really need to do is to envision myself at that perfect size or that perfect weight.....and hypnosis will help me get there easily and effortlessly, just like magic.

I know that weight loss really comes down to a simple math equation.......I need to expend more energy than I take in......and that's it. Once I adhere to this process, I will lose all the weight I desire, easily and effortlessly.

I now see myself standing in front of a three-way mirror. There is no one here but me, so I have no need to be shy. In this magical mirror, it's easy to see myself at my ideal size and weight.

I think about that perfect number.....my weight loss goal. I also know in this very relaxed state of mind.....I always want to focus on the state of mind or state of health I am working towards.......not the state of mind I am coming from.

Again.....I focus on that ideal number for me ......and I notice how the mirror portrays meat this perfect size and weight just like that. This is an effortless process because anything is possible with the power of my amazing subconscious mind.

As I look into this mirror, I enjoy seeing yourself at my ideal size and weight, having already achieved my weight loss goal......and I like what you see. Again, I focus on that number, my ideal weight or size........this is my magic number. As you think about this number or size, I silently repeat in my mind:

I am now my perfect size....and again, I repeat in my mind what that size is.

I am now my perfect size....

I am now my perfect weight.

I am now my perfect weight.

It's so easy to be healthy.

As I look in the mirror, my muscles are toned and tight........my thighs are slim, even my abdomen is flat. I look and feel incredible.

Every day I focus on this healthy image of myself............I imagine myself standing in front of this three-way mirror, at my absolutely perfect weight and size.

I know that part of being healthy means developing healthy lifestyle habits ......and I am ready to make that all important commitment.

I am ready to live longer and to live better. I am now enjoying a superb level of both physical and mental health and well-being and I am ready to make any changes necessary in support of this weight loss goal.

I know that everything I am or everything I will ever be is the result of those choices and decisions I make. If I want to change some aspect of my life, I simply need to make new choices and new decisions. I am disciplined and follow through with those choices and decisions.

Being healthy is a matter of choice, and I am choosing good health today. I eat less and exercise more, you find it is quite easy to manage my weight.

I eat the right foods, in the right proportions at the right times.

Now that I am at my perfect size and weight, I have more energy and more mental clarity. I have achieved my ideal weight, effortlessly and I know that this helps me other areas of life, because it makes everything easier and much more manageable.

Now that I have developed these healthy lifestyle habits, I now look at food as fuel..........I now realize that just like an engine that runs more efficiently with the proper fuel, so does my body.

I like looking and feeling healthy, and even find myself craving healthy foods.

I now avoid those foods that are not part of a healthy diet like sweets, sugar and fast foods and fried foods. I know these types of foods are not part of a healthy lifestyle and I simply have no desire for them and as a matter of fact, my body rejects these types of foods because I know they are inefficient and ineffective.

I naturally gravitate towards healthy foods and even find I love exercising and moving your body, each and every day.

I now give myself permission to stay at this healthy weight, because I like what I see. I now allow myself to lose as much weight as I need to achieve that perfectly toned body. I know I deserve to be healthy and I deserve to be happy and fulfilled, in every area of life, especially my health.

As I enjoy these amazing feelings, I repeat in my mind:

I easily achieve and maintain my ideal weight.

I am easily satisfied with just a small amount of food.

I have a naturally high metabolism.

I am the picture of good health.

For me, weight loss is effortless process.

I am now my perfect size, I am now my perfect size.

I now see myself several months down the road, still looking and feeling fantastic. I notice how much my life has improved. Everyone wants to know what my secret is, and I simply smile and tell them, I don't know, weight loss just became easy!

These suggestions have now become permanently embedded into my subconscious mind, and they are now part of my actions, my behavior and my personality from this moment forward.

As I count from 1 - 5 I will return to conscious awareness.

Number 1......coming back slowly.

Number 2........a little more now.

Number 3..........coming back to the present time and the present place.

Number 4......excited about all of these incredible changes.

Number 5.....eyes open, wide awake. Eyes open, wide awake.

Pack on Muscle with Ease

Simply repeat the following statements to relax.

The deeper I go the better I feel and the better I feel the deeper I go. I allow the soothing sound of my voice to calm and relax me. Moment by moment, my mind is becoming as clear as the surface of a calm and quiet lake. As I continue to breathe deeply, I become more and more relaxed, more and more at ease.

I allow my body to become more and more relaxed with each passing moment. Every sound that I hear allows me to go deeper and deeper into hypnotic trance. It's easy for me to relax deeply.

Breathing deeply brings me into a deep state of relaxation. I am at peace.

I am calm and relaxed. I easily achieve a very deep state of relaxation. Each and every muscle of my body is now relaxing.

I see myself as a powerful and strong person. I pack on muscle with ease.

I am strong, I am muscular.

When I walk down the street, people notice me. I have a wonderful physique. It's easy for me to develop and build muscle. I enjoy building my muscles. Everything I do in life supports a strong and healthy body.

I am strong, I am muscular.

When I exercise and work out, I easily build muscle. I am strong and lean. Even the foods I eat support my healthy muscular body.

It's easy for me to visualize my strong muscular body. I like visualizing myself lean and strong. When I look in the mirror, I see a strong healthy, muscular body. It's easy for me to pack on muscles.

I can see myself in the mirror, flexing my muscles. My arms and legs are strong. My abdomen is lean and muscular. I maintain a healthy body, because of my lean, strong muscles.

Because I am muscular and strong, I easily maintain my healthy weight. The foods I eat support a healthy body.

I am strong, I am muscular.

I like showing off my lean, muscular body, because I am proud of what I have accomplished. I think of myself of a healthy person. I have a lean, strong body. I am the picture of good health, and it shows.

It's easy for me to maintain my strong healthy body. I love working out. I love lifting weights. I like finding new ways to build muscle. It's an effortless process.

From this moment forward, I pack on muscles with ease, and it so.

I am strong, I am muscular.

I now see myself several months down the road, still looking and feeling fantastic. I notice how much my life has improved. Everyone wants to know what my secret is, and I simply smile and tell them, I don't know, packing on muscles just became easy.

These suggestions have now become permanently embedded into my subconscious mind, and they are now part of my actions, my behavior and my personality from this moment forward.

As I count from 1 - 5 I will return to conscious awareness.

Number 1......coming back slowly.

45

Number 2........a little more now.

Number 3..........coming back to the present time and the present place.

Number 4......excited about all of these incredible changes.

Number 5.....eyes open, wide awake. Eyes open, wide awake.

Living in a Positive Perspective

Begin by relaxing and getting into a comfortable position. Just read the script out loud allowing your words to flow into your consciousness.

Feeling a sense of peace, I allow the soothing sound of my voice to lull me into a sort of hypnotic trance. I am speaking softly and slowly, as I go deeper and deeper into this beautiful state of trance. My voice and my body are slowing down, as though everything is in slow motion. With every word I speak, and every sound I make, I go deeper and deeper into a state of hypnotic trance. Moment by moment, my mind is becoming clearer and clearer, as smooth as the surface of a beautiful lake.

As my mind clears I know, *I always think positively.*

I use my imagination to relax even more deeply. As I speak, I imagine myself walking along a beautiful beach.

As I walk, I can hear the sounds of the waves hitting the shore and I can feel the sea breeze as it touches my nose. I take deep and cleansing breaths, which helps me go deeper and deeper into this beautiful relaxation.

I feel the sea breeze drift over my body, and I notice the sun as it warms my skin. The sun touches me wherever I have tension or stress, instantly dissolving anything it finds. This beautiful healing light allows me to go even deeper into this beautiful sense of relaxation. All of my stress and tension is now dissolving, as I go deeper and deeper. Every time I speak the words, deeper and deeper, I will go into a deep state of hypnotic trance.

I feel myself moving deeper and deeper down, as I begin to count backward from five to one.

Number five.........I feel very calm and relaxed.

Number four........I'm moving down deeper and deeper.

Number three......deeper still.

Number two...........I feel myself descending ever deeper now. And on the next number, I will drift into a very deep state of relaxation. And......

Number one...........I am in a very deep state of relaxation, and I am ready to make some amazing changes in my life.

I always think positively.

I am now deeply relaxed.......and ready to make some amazing changes in my life. Being positive is a lot more fun than being negative, so from this moment on **I always think positively.**

It's easy to think positively, so I naturally gravitate towards it. I know my brain is simply a reflection of my thoughts, so I always think in a positive manner. Enthusiasm makes life a whole lot more fun. It's like having inner sunshine; it makes me more likeable and even more attractive. Enthusiasm is probably one of the most attractive qualities I can have. When I am eager and enthusiastic everyone I come in contact with feels it. I am just more fun to be round.

I always think in a positive manner, and as a matter of fact, I can turn any situation into something positive. I know that every person, place or thing in my life is meant to teach me something.

I feel a new energy and enthusiasm towards life, and it shows. This feeling of excitement and exuberance colors everything I say and do. I am overflowing with an eager anticipation and enjoyment for life.

I am taking this new zest for life and changing the world with my style and my pizazz and your passion. Enthusiasm and positivity is one of the greatest natural resources I have, and I am overflowing with it. It's a natural talent and it makes everything more interesting and more productive and more successful.

I imagine waking up in the future, just feeling fantastic. I think about how I spend my day, now that I have everything I want. I just feel good about life, because everything goes my way. I am in the flow of life, and I everything in my life has improved because of my new attitude.

My energy is uplifting, and everyone loves me. It's so easy to be positive.

I always think positively.

My presence in the room makes people smile. I rise to the challenge, because I always feel positive.

- I have the power to transform my life.

- I feel inspired each and every day.

- I am naturally enthusiastic and joyful.

- My enthusiasm is contagious.

- I feel great every day.

- I am filled with awe and wonder.

- I always think positively.

I now see myself several months down the road, still looking and feeling fantastic. I notice how much my life has improved.

These suggestions have now become permanently embedded into my subconscious mind, and they are now part of my actions, my behavior and my personality from this moment forward.

As I count from 1 - 5 I will return to conscious awareness.

Number 1......coming back slowly.

Number 2........a little more now.

Number 3..........coming back to the present time and the present place.

Number 4......excited about all of these incredible changes.

Number 5.....eyes open, wide awake. Eyes open, wide awake.

Boost Confidence Through the Roof

Begin by relaxing and getting into a comfortable position. Just read the script out loud allowing your words to flow into your consciousness.

Feeling a sense of peace, I allow the soothing sound of my voice to lull me into a sort of hypnotic trance. I am speaking softly and slowly, as I go deeper and deeper into this beautiful state of trance. My voice and my body are slowing down, as though everything is in slow motion. With every word I speak, and every sound I make, I go deeper and deeper into a state of hypnotic trance. Moment by moment, my mind is becoming clearer and clearer, as smooth as the surface of a beautiful lake.

As my mind clears I know, *I feel confident, I am confident.*

I use my imagination to relax even more deeply. As I speak, I imagine myself walking along a beautiful beach.

As I walk, I can hear the sounds of the waves hitting the shore and I can feel the sea breeze as it touches my nose. I take deep and cleansing breaths, which helps me go deeper and deeper into this beautiful relaxation.

I feel the sea breeze drift over my body, and I notice the sun as it warms my skin. The sun touches me wherever I have tension or stress, instantly dissolving anything it finds. This beautiful healing light allows me to go even deeper into this beautiful sense of relaxation. All of my stress and tension is now dissolving, as I go deeper and deeper. Every time I speak the words, deeper and deeper, I will go into a deep state of hypnotic trance.

I feel myself moving deeper and deeper down, as I begin to count backward from five to one.

Number five.........I feel very calm and relaxed.

Number four........I'm moving down deeper and deeper.

Number three......deeper still.

Number two...........I feel myself descending ever deeper now. And on the next number, I will drift into a very deep state of relaxation. And......

Number one...........I am in a very deep state of relaxation, and I am ready to make some amazing changes in my life.

I feel confident, I am confident.

I am now deeply relaxed.......and ready to make some amazing changes in my life. As I walk along the beach, I notice an area on the sand where words are written. I walk a little closer, and realize these are words I used to use to describe myself.

Since I am now a very confident person, I have no use for these old words that used to describe how I felt about myself. As I stare at these words, the water suddenly washes up over them, erasing them from the sand.

I am inspired to write down some new words, but this time I carve them into a rock sitting nearby. The words I choose to write to describe myself are words like:

Confident, caring, compassionate, successful, loving, joyful, prosperous, abundant, and truly amazing.

As I relax, I think of even more words I might carve into this rock....and I repeat those words silently in my mind.

I feel powerful and full of life, and it shows. I have amazing confidence, and I feel it from deep within. This newfound confidence begins to open new doors and new opportunities for me, and I feel amazing.

As I reflect on this new mindset I repeat to myself:

- I have a new sense of confidence and joy.

- I have a new energy and vitality for life.

- I deserve the best that life has to offer.

- Everything in my life is improving because of my amazing confidence.

- I am amazing and I am worth the effort.

- I am strong.

- I feel confident, I am confident.

I now realize that I deserve the best that life has to offer and I feel a new vitality and energy for life. I have a new sense of confidence. I feel comfortable in my own skin I have an amazing sense of style and purpose. I feel a huge sense of relief. I feel as if a heavy weight has been lifted. My spirit begins to soar.

I feel a great sense of respect for myself, and as a result of this new self-respect I have a new air of confidence. I feel as if I could achieve and accomplish anything now....and it shows.

I exude confidence. ***I feel confident, I am confident.***

I now see myself several months down the road, still looking and feeling fantastic.

These suggestions have now become permanently embedded into my subconscious mind, and they are now part of my actions, my behavior and my personality from this moment forward.

As I count from 1 - 5 I will return to conscious awareness.

Number 1......coming back slowly.

Number 2........a little more now.

Number 3..........coming back to the present time and the present place.

Number 4......excited about all of these incredible changes.

Number 5.....eyes open, wide awake. Eyes open, wide awake.

Making Self-Hypnosis A Daily Habit

Learning how to do self-hypnosis can literally transform your life, and in this book you learned the steps you can take to get there. Self-hypnosis is an absolutely incredible tool that can be used to improve any area of life.

The best way to use self-hypnosis is to make it a daily habit. There is no limit to the imagination. Hypnosis can take you on an amazing journey and help you accomplish incredible things. The only limit you have is within your own mind.

There have been many studies, which have shown the effectiveness of hypnosis including one done by the infamous Harvard Medical School in 1999, which published a report on the study of hypnosis on broken bones. The study involved 12 participants who had broken ankles, half of which received the typical treatment and the other half receiving hypnosis once a week for 12 weeks.

The results indicated that those who underwent hypnosis healed significantly faster than those undergoing typical treatment. Those in the hypnosis group healed an equivalent of eight and a half weeks six weeks after the fractures (Harvard Medical School, 1999). Many attribute the success of hypnosis to the placebo effect but there are arguments for and against this.

Ohio State University (2004) researchers did studies that determined that related relaxation and hypnosis can help prevent the weakening of an immune response that normally follows times of acute stress with studies showing that hypnosis enhanced the immune status of a select group of people when compared to those that did not undergo hypnosis.

These kinds of findings with further research could have a significant effect on medicine in the future, specifically for patients healing from surgeries. The British Psychological Society (UK, 2001), stated that there is actually convincing evidence that chronic and acute pain caused by medical and dental procedures and childbirth can be relieved with hypnosis.

But what about the brain in all of this, what kind of studies do we have that show brain imagining in terms of hypnosis you might ask?

Milling (2008) investigated several studies utilizing various brain imagining technologies such as neuroimaging techniques like positron emission tomography and functional magnetic resonance imaging when looking at the effects of hypnosis on the brain. One study suggested that hypnotic suggestions actually caused " increased blood flow to the frontal cortices, as well as the medial and lateral posterior parietal cortices" (Milling, p. 173).

Another study showed that showed that "hypnosis reduced both the intensity and unpleasantness of the pain, and was modulated by activity in a region of the anterior cingulate cortex called the midcingulate cortex" (Milling, p. 173). These are certainly promising studies that show the science can indeed begin to postulate that hypnosis does in fact altar the chemistry of the brain.

Fingelkurts, Fingelkurts, Kallio & Reveonssuo (2007) have shown that hypnosis actually induces a changed composition in brain oscillations in EEG studies with the EEG during hypnosis differing from the non-hypnotic state, specifically in the frontal lobe of the brain.

When it comes down to it, researchers have made great strides in looking at the effectiveness of hypnosis, and with more and more interest in the field, the future looks bright.

References:

British Psychological Society (UK, 2001)

http://www.bps.org.uk/downloadfile.cfm?file_uuid=A7AF6
617-1143-DFD0-7E14-10B42D589040&ext=pdf

Harvard Medical School (USA, 1999)

http://www.news.harvard.edu/gazette/2003/05.08/01-
hypnosis.html

Milling, L. S. (2008). Recent developments in the study of hypnotic pain reduction: a new golden era of research? *Contemporary Hypnosis (John Wiley & Sons, Inc.)*, 25(3/4), 165- 177. doi:10.1002/ch.362

Ohio State University (USA, 2004)

http://researchnews.osu.edu/archive/hypnosis.htm

Conclusion

Congratulations!

You have everything you need to begin the process of self-hypnosis. Hypnosis is a very powerful tool and it can help you make some incredible changes in your life. I hope you have enjoyed learning a little bit more about self-hypnosis and how you can use it in your every day life to make long-lasting changes.

Hypnosis can change your life, in a manner of speaking, because it can help you change your thoughts at the subconscious level. If you have never tried it, I would encourage you to do so, just remember to start small and work on one thing at a time.

The next step is to start using these tips and scripts in your everyday life!

Thank you and good luck!

~G.S Dhoot

Printed in Great Britain
by Amazon.co.uk, Ltd.,
Marston Gate.